The Bureaucratic Zoo

The Bureaucratic Zoo
The Search For The Ultimate Mumble

James H. Boren (Mr. Mumbles)

Photographs by Joseph Beggun

EPM Publications, Inc.
McLean, Virginia

Library of Congress Cataloging in Publication Data

Boren, James H.
    The bureaucratic zoo.

    1. Bureaucracy—Anecdotes, facetiae, satire, etc.
I. Beggun, Joseph.   II. Title.
JF1601.B657   301.18'32'0207   76-39967
ISBN 0-914440-14-4

Published in McLean, Virginia, 1003 Turkey Run Road,
by EPM Publications, Inc.
and in Toronto, Canada, by Van Nostrand Reinhold Ltd.

Printed in the United States of America

Photographs by David A.D. Wilson on pages 3, 10, 40, 43, 85, 114
and 115, by Ann Genett for *TWA Ambassador* on page 73
and by Stan Jennings on page 52

Design by Melanson Associates

With a special tip of the hat to...

Red Buck, the Chief
Zippy, the Chimp
Hugo, the Singing Bull Mastiff
Ding, the Black Cat
Tiger, the Ginger Cat
Helen, Cathy, Una, Minnie, Marilyn, and
Those Bureaucrats whose hands are tied
*   by outmoded rules and regulations*
*   but who fight the good fight*
*   for responsive public service.*

Typing by Hilary A. Hottle on an IBM Selectric Typewriter
Model No. 71, Adjutant Ball!!

The processing of the film and printing was done under the
direction of Joseph Beggun by Executive Photo Corporation
of Silver Spring, Maryland.

Contents

introduction

Early in its years of development, the bureaucratic movement was conceived, born, and nurtured in much the same manner that characterizes governmental bureaucracy today. Being pressed close to the public breast, wrapped in the protective swaddling clothes of red tape, and residuating[1] in an ever-growing nest of memoranda and shreddistic materials, the governmental bureaucrats have been the pioneers in developing new ways of doing nothing, and thereby preserving the creative *status quo* for which the bureaucratic movement is known.[2]

Bureaucracy, however, is no longer the province of public servants only. Corporate, academic, religious, union, professional, association, and foundation bureaucrats have been captured by the spirit of bold irresolution.[3] They are reacting in an increasingly nonresponsive manner to their respective publics. Bureaucracy, therefore, is not the domain of any particular group. *Bureaucracy is a way of life.*

In the animal kingdom, the patterns of behavior are undergoing subtle changes which tend to harmonize man's

---

1. **To residuate:** A Borenverb. To burrow into a fixed immovable position while maintaining a low profile. Residuation is a survival practice often used during changes of administration.

2. **Bureaucratic Movement** (BM): The spread or movement of bureaucracy from the body politic or the body corporate. Usually called "the bureaucratic movement" in capital cities, but known in the countryside as "the BM of Ottawa" or "the BM of Washington."

3. The term bureaucrat was once used to refer to employees of governmental bureaus, but today it is used to apply to anyone who uses orbital dialogues and profundification of ideas, if any, and to anyone who interfaces dynamic inaction and procedural abstractions in order to implement retrogressive thrusts. To a bureaucrat, it is not the results that count, it is the procedures; substantive action is the necessary evil that permits the development of procedures, forms, and hiring of more people.

bureaucratic progress with the life style of his fellow creatures. Insecticides used in the rural areas have driven the surviving birds to the cities where, instead of seeking the insects of the fields and forests, they hover around backyard feeders or flutter around park benches. Dogs once foraged in the countryside or lunged for table scraps, but today their snarls and snaps are heard as they protect the expensive food served to them in specially designed plastic bowls. Bears once carved their domain from the marshes and forests in which they lived, but now their snorts and roars are heard as they proclaim their sovereignty over garbage cans in parks and campgrounds. And man continues to institutionalize his daily life while carving out little domains through the use of organizational charts, clearance authority, memo drafting, and regulatory forms. Social processes become more and more intricate, and simplicity becomes more and more profundified.[4]

Zoologists and social scientists may ultimately find a blending of their professional areas of studies, for truly all the world is a stage . . . and the stage is a gigantic zoo.

The word "zoo" conjures to mind small cages, iron bars, moats, and railings which restrict the lives of so-called strange and exotic creatures to be gawked at by a fellow creature, man. Zoos are undergoing significant change, however; open zoos and ranging preserves are being de-

---

4. **To profundify or to profundicate:**A Borenverb used to denote the use of thesauric and other enrichment techniques to make a simple idea appear to be profound. Profundification and profundication mean the same thing; the distinction is in the origin of use. Graduates of agricultural institutions tend to use "to profundicate" while graduates of ivy league schools tend to use "to profundify."

veloped in order that the caged ones can appear to have greater freedom and more naturalness in their controlled lives. Man is becoming the caged one who shuttles by buses or barred passageways through the larger animal arenas in order to gawk, take pictures, and slyly toss popcorn and peanuts to those on the other side.

As the open zoo concept grows, man and his colleagues may sense a greater range of physical freedom. More parks, more campgrounds, more waterways, more ski slopes, and more hiking and biking trails will facilitate the exercise of random movement. The physical cages will give way to institutional restraints that may be invisible and, therefore, more acceptable.

Who cares about more and more agencies of government at all levels creating more and more forms to be completed as long as the ski slopes are open and the waterways are available for sailing? Why worry about secret agents developing files on one's daily life as long as the beaches are open and the garbage is collected at camp sites? Who cares about foreign policy and the little international war games as long as the chair is comfortable, the beer is cold, and the television commercials are occasionally interrupted by the broadcast of sporting events or shoot-'em-up movies? Of what real concern is it to an individual that the institutions that once served have become the institutions that now command?

Ah, but these are far too serious questions to pose as we prepare for a leisurely stroll through the bureaucratic zoo. Let us prepare ourselves for the stroll by semi-yogifying our minds and bodies.

Let us close our eyes. Let us mentally float on flatuous clouds of ethereal bliss, and let us quietly but reverently intone the incantations of the eternal verities of the bureau-cratic way:

Red tape is the tape that binds the world into a great cohesive unit. Dah, dah, de dah dah.

Bureaucrats are not opposed to cutting red tape as long as it is cut lengthwise. Hum, hum, duh humboog.

Happiness in a bureaucracy is a scratched back. Tah, tah, te tah tah.

If you are going to be a phoney, be sincere about it. Thrum, thrum, oh thrum thrum.

Bureaucrats are never wrong about their positions on issues; they simply adjust the issues to fit their positions, if any. Ay, ay, ee eye eyeeee.

Study a problem long enough, and it will go away. Sh, sh, ah sh sh.

Bureaucrats do not need language . . . only words. Blah, blah, ah blaw blaw.

Crisis is the culture in which bureaucracies grow. Um, um, oh um um.

Pornography to a bureaucrat is a blank sheet of paper. Shuf, shuf, oh shuf shuf.

More ideas are killed by yesbuttisms than by logic. Ya, ya, ha ya ya.
Thrum, thrum, oh thrum thrum.
Sh, sh, ah sh sh.

Bureaucrats are collectively the ultimate repository of national values. Ow, ow, oh ow ow.

When in charge, ponder. When in trouble, delegate. When in doubt, mumble. Mm, mm, blah mm mm.

From the quiet mind-drift and the satisfying mental vacuity that billow forth from these preparatory incantations, let us be inspired to begin our self-strokistic stroll along the path of the bureaucratic zoo. Let us gaze upon a few of the world's bureaucrats as some swing from one trapeze to another while others sleep peacefully on the lower rungs of career ladders.

Let us observe political newcomers as they pace within their cages with flamboyant gestures and eloquent snorts. And we may joyfully watch the pacing colleague who collects those snorts to recast them with flaquistic artistry, and who then projects them into the echo chambers of the body politic. May we also watch the bureaucrats respond to those snorts with the gelatinal movement that proclaims action but whose visible quivering never disturbs the immovable base of the bureaucracy.

Let us gaze upon a few of the world's bureaucrats, and let us shed an occasional tear of moderated joy and escapistic acquiescence as we accept our role as servants to the servants. For, truly, the P.T. Barnum philosophy of public service is the basis on which the greatest zoo is built . . . and its efficacy assures that the zoo will never close.[5]

[5] There's a sucker born every minute.

- *P.T. Barnum*

Let's Fingertap Together

Let's fingertap together
In a dedicated way,
And postpone all decisions
Until another day.

Let's orchestrate and dialogue
In words that we adore,
The words that we've all mumbled
A million times or more.

Let's shuffle all our paper,
And fuzzify our minds;
Let's wrap our brains in cobwebs,
And love red tape that binds.

Let's regulate the people
With rules, reports, and forms;
Inspire true innovation
As long as it conforms.

Let's optimize the *status quo*,
And sit right where we are,
For if we keep our profile low,
We'll get no battle scar.

Let's cut our red tape lengthwise,
Profundicate our words,
And build great stacks of paper
The stuff that undergirds.

Yes, let's fingertap together
In a dedicated way,
And postpone all decisions
Until another day.

leadership

When a taxpayer hears the word "leadership," he or she may think of a Teddy Roosevelt dashing up San Juan Hill with sword flashing in the sun and shouting words of encouragement to his men. Thoughts may turn to a Franklin Roosevelt whose fireside chats gave hope to a people who struggled to rebuild a nation, or to a Winston Churchill who inspired a weary and embattled people to new heights of courage. Such concepts of leadership, however, are not appropriate to the more complex world of today, for individual leadership has been replaced by institutionalized committees, and the substantive factors of leadership have been replaced by the more realistic elements of image.

Successful leaders in corporate, academic, and governmental bureaucracies are those who are able to sustain the leadership image through a variety of proven techniques. Leaders in all bureaucracies know how to use appropriate status symbols, how to assume an authoritative air, how to project full and resonant tonal patterns, how to occasionally adopt the friendly but condescending "buddy" role, and how to make the underlings who do whatever work is done feel wanted and important.

Leadership in the bureaucratic zoo, therefore, is not based upon ability to perform but is based upon the ability to appear to perform. It involves the roar, not the message; the studies, not the conclusions; the procedures, not the results; and the image, not the reality.

Most bureaucrats at the supernal levels enjoy looking at the "big picture," for it is the overview that is important, and it is the overview that removes the administrator from the actual work of the organization. Administrative leaders never work; they globate.[1] By looking at the globalities, one can avoid not only working with details but also the need to learn much about them. Also, by dealing with the global scene, there are no corners into which the leader may be trapped.

Bureaucratic leadership is essentially orbitalogical in nature . . . that is, it is neither logical nor illogical, but it is leadership that goes in pulsating circles as it moves between that which is logical and that which is illogical. Bureaucratic mutation may occasionally give rise to fresh ideas, but they are quickly ingested with amoebic procedures and modified with peristaltic finality.

What are some of the marginal thoughts about leadership that one may find today? Let us shuffle about in one small corner of the bureaucratic zoo, and with half-open eyes and ringing ears learn of what marginalities we can.

1. **To globate.** A Borenverb which denotes circular motion through all planes. Bureaucrats thus may globate as a means of giving a geometrical touch to their spherical movements.

If you can't beat them, don't just join them;
lead them.

Bureaucrats never change the course of the ship of state.
They simply adjust the compass.

*Being a leader in a bureaucracy depends less on golden
ability than brassy spirit. The bureaucratic leaders,
of course, are always second in line, because they shove
someone else out front to test the water. The one out front
usually bears the title of Special Assistant.*

If you don't have anything to do, do it with style.
Dynamic inaction with style is a key to bureaucratic success.

To evaluate the pull of a bureaucrat, one must know
the levers that he can pull.

A bureaucratic leader is one whose radii expand and contract to produce pulsating circularity of thought and action. Such leadership is the basis of creative nonresponsiveness and bold irresolution.

Budgetary Superiority is the measure of
Bureaucratic Success.   BS = BS.

Pomposity is the seat of bureaucratic power.

*They called him one of the most imaginative men
in the country — just before they passed sentence.*

communications

If it hasn't been said before, don't say it now; nothing should be said or done for the first time.

If one is forced to say something, however, one should proliferate the verbalities and maximize the adjectivations in order to profundify, trashify, and fuzzify what is said.[1] Such an approach enables the dedicated bureaucrat to say nothing while seeming to have said something informative and profound.

Communications, therefore, can be very dangerous if a thought or message is conveyed, but communications can be safe if the communicator knows how to transmit a feeling of well-being without transmitting information, giving a position on an issue, or making a commitment of any type. It is the form, not the substance, that is important in bureaucratic communication.

A mayor can communicate deep concern about a problem and turn away the wrath of an angry delegation of citizens by appointing a Blue Ribbon Commission.[2] A member of Congress can thank a constituent for his views but avoid a commitment by stating that "the final form of the bill

1. For profundify see page 4, for trashify, see page 38, for fuzzify, read any page of any copy of the Congressional Record.
2. Blue Ribbon Commissions are simply committees which, like most committees, task forces, and other advisory or study groups, are used not to find solutions to problems or to recommend specific lines of action but to postpone the day when a controversial issue must be faced. If a problem is studied long enough, it may go away. Historians of the Bureaucratic Movement (BM) have not been able to determine the reason for the use of the color "Blue" as applied to Ribbon Commissions. Regardless of the title, most taxpayers in Canada and the United States view Blue Ribbon Commissions to be what they really are, Red Tape Commissions.

will not be known until it comes to the floor for action." A corporate president can "communicate" with stockholders at the annual meeting, but avoid giving information through trashifying the response with irrelevant material and profundifying the response with statistics. A university president can avoid questions posed by appropriation committee members by academifying the philosophical bottom line.[3]

The most characteristic of all communicative techniques is that of professional mumbling, and the basic rule of bureaucrats at both the top and bottom of the ladder is, "When in doubt, mumble."

Fullness of sound, roundness of vowels, and resonance of tone, the style of all creatures in the bureaucratic zoo meets with broad acceptance with the public. Vertical and linear mumbling can help profundify and fuzzify the non-directive communication without making the nondirectiveness apparent.[4] And as students of the bureaucratic zoo know, the geo-cultural factors have been recognized as important influences on minimal wordations. In Canada, for example, the simple expression "eh" (pronounced as a long A) is similar to the Germanic " ja," the Spanish "pues," and

3. At the national level, some members of Congress become lost in philosophical discussions, but they have demonstrated a certain grasp of the bottom line concept, though more physical than fiscal.

4. Vertical mumbling is the interfacing of multiphonic word strings with authoritative intonations; linear mumbling is the translocation of tonal patterns with an occasional surfacing of a word or phrase. For more information on the technique of mumbling with verticality or linearity, see Boren, *When in Doubt, Mumble* (New York, Van Nostrand Reinhold, 1972) or Boren, *Have Your Way With Bureaucrats* (Philadelphia, Chilton Book Company, 1975). Eh, ja, pues, huh, mm!

the American "huh." The English "mm," however, has broader implications for minimal thought wordation, because it is traceable to the light gruntifying of King George III. Specifically translated, each minimal wordation can mean: yes, no, maybe, don't bother me now, yes-but, how great, interesting, don't give me that, whaddayaknow, and don't you agree.

Whereas minimal wordations are primarily geo-cultural in nature, the haughticality and gruntification factors of communications are essentially social in nature. Those creatures that are high in the social structure of the bureaucratic zoo tend to be outstanding in their ability to speak with haughticality, but they can also gruntify if absolutely necessary. Gruntification is commonly practiced by "the working stiffs" of the bureaucratic zoo.

To speak with haughticality, bureaucratic creatures stretch their bodies to a fully upright position, lift their chins to the point that the base is horizontal or parallel to the surface of any nearby table, and project their words or sounds by constricting the diaphragm. One can induce haughticality by poking a bureaucrat in the stomach area, but such haughticality may lack the proper nasalisms. Haughtical nasalisms are not essential to haughtication, but they are helpful in putting the final touch to the high-class art. The outstanding nasal haughticators are those who haughticate while constricting the nasal passages as if smelling something bad. Beginning haughticators sometimes practice the art by forcefully pressing their stomachs with their hands while uttering words or sounds. Most of the world's distinguished haughticators can be found among ambassadors, critics, senators and practicing snobs.

Gruntifying is a special projection of serious emphasis; that is, if a creature wishes to bear down on an issue, it wrinkles his or her forehead, constricts the muscles not only in the stomach region but also in the colonic area, and gruntifies the words through the voice box. It is never used in levity.

Beginners should exercise caution as they learn to gruntify. First gruntifications should be done in privacy, because accidents sometimes occur.

A mumble can never be quoted.

Bureaucrats are the only people in the world who can say absolutely nothing and mean it.

*When a bureaucrat makes a mistake and continues
to make it, it usually becomes the new policy.*

A dynamic bureaucrat is one who gestures vigorously while saying nothing.

His mind itches and his heart twitches
as he longs for a beautiful mumble.

A successful bureaucrat is one who can draft memos or "position papers" to cover all posibilities.

Successful bureaucrats are poor lip kissers.

Bureaucratic eloquence consists of mumbling in forceful and resonant tones. That is, to speak with maximized effervescence of marginal thought patterns as interfaced with the viable options of nondirective interdigitation.

Thundering indignation wins more arguments than the quiet voice of logic.

To inflatuate: A Hottlistic verb form. *To introduce flatuous or flatuatory overtones to communications or to communicators. (Flatuatory pomposity is the essence of bureaucracy.)*

To fuzzify: A Borenverb. *To present a matter in terms that permit adjustive interpretation. Particularly useful when the fuzzifier does not know what he or she is talking about, or when the fuzzifier wants to enunciate a non-position in the form of a position.*

To trashify: A Borenverb. *To use unrelated or nonessential information in verbal or written communications.*

Trashification is often used by politicians, academicians, and governmental bureaucrats to demonstrate in-depth knowledge in fields of marginal value. Profundifiers and fuzzifiers usually enjoy trashifying, but trashifiers are happiest when digging for secondary and tertiary material with which to enrich the refuse of their communications.

Some try to keep the lid on their principal source of information.

political orbits

There was once a myth, now practically forgotten, that the people of a nation have a right to know something about the people's business. Another myth held that elected representatives of the people would reflect the will of the people in matters of public policy. The relationship of myth and history is of interest to scholars and to some taxpayers. The distinction is sometimes fuzzy, however, and becomes lost in the interfacing of complementary legends and unclassified memoranda.

The history of parliamentary governments indicates that the concept of representative government is a viable one—but the matter of who is represented has undergone significant change through the process of contributory fiscalities and institutional evolution. At one time, people with common interests would work on common problems as individuals but as the common interests gave rise to non-public bureaucracies, people with common interests transferred their cash and delegated the political expression of their power to vote to the new bureaucracies. Thus began the Era of Accommodation.

The legislative branch of government now rarely confronts the functionaries in the executive branch, and the executive branch has learned to accommodate itself to the desires of legislators and the staffs who do the menial work to carry out the parliamentary will. The lobby branch serves as an amalgam that orchestrates the diversity of interests and also serves as the epoxy to fiscalize the direction of policy. The Era of Accommodation thus finds harmony among the mythological balancers, and the individual who once had influence through the vote now finds it easier to acquiesce.

When the three dollar bill is established, the politicians will design it, the bureaucrats will spend it, and the taxpayers will bear it.

The circle of accommodation will be completed when the taxpayers finally fold their tents and accept bureaucrats as their guardian angels. Politicians and bureaucrats are functional twins. They communicate the same way; they work at the same rate; and they produce the same results. The taxpayers, wearying under the load of the Accommodation, may be tempted to play the game of funny money, and join the politicians and bureaucrats who believe that the national treasury is propped up by the Great Tooth Fairy.

Ahhhh! (Let us whisper, please.) What will happen when the Great Tooth Fairy gazes upon the last of the taxpayers' teeth?

Shall we wander back to the Bureaucratic Zoo? And find another Living Gimmick to take the place of the Great Tooth Fairy?

Some politicians have their own concept of the free enterprise system. That is, their services are sold to the highest bidder.

43

Successful politicians and bureaucrats share the ability to marginate or hover while sensing the will of their bosses. Sensitive antennae pick up the grumblings of the electorate or the desires of the bureaucratic superiors. The politicians and bureaucrats can then leap boldly into the ranks of marginal leaders.

All mumblers are not bureaucrats — some are members of Congress or the House of Commons.

Political Bureaucrats (POLIBUS). *Politicians are bureaucrats at heart. They do not deal in forms, but they deal in thousands of non-question questionnaires with which they update their mailing lists. They lovingly shuffle their index cards listing supporters and they "buck" constituent mail to agency bureaucrats for noncommittal answers that will be transmitted with a noncommittal letter to the constituent in the hope of obtaining a commitment for political support.*

While political biographers are among the best fiction writers of the world, government information officers and politicians are the most outstanding orbital dialoguers of the world. The orbital dialogues are most effectively presented during press conferences when pseudo-crises are described in profound terms and analyzed with nondirective logic.

It is difficult to determine the position of a politician by what he says — even if one knows the longitude and platitude of his speeches.

Politicians and bureaucrats usually create an offal situation.

A moderate is one who is looking for a safe place to land.

thought patterns

The thought patterns of some bureaucrats have been described as embodying boldness, resoluteness, and brilliance. Of course, those are the descriptions of hired flaques. Nevertheless, the thought patterns of some bureaucrats tend to be intricate tracings of magnificent old lace. Intricate, looping, circular, and often held together by more starch than textile . . . these are some of the characteristics of the lace-oriented thought patterns. Some bureaucrats, however, have thought patterns that are more flaky than lacy.

To attempt to trace the thought patterns of bureaucrats would be totally devoid of wisdom. A few characteristics of bureaucratic thought patterns may be described, however, in order that puzzled taxpayers may have a more appreciative attitude toward those whom they pay to command them.[1]

Bureaucrats are magnificent in the manner in which they prodigiously ponder all factors, all interrelationships, all near-relationships, all non-related factors, and other factoral relationships as they make tentative approaches to preliminary plans for initiating feasibility studies on the possibilities of planning future study conferences on the subject of decision-making.

To observe a bureaucrat who is deep in thought is a tranquil and restful experience, but it can be embarrassing to both the "thinker" and the observer if the bureaucrat is part

---

1. The taxpayer-bureaucrat relationship can be described as fiscal sadism. That is, the taxpayers pay the taxes to pay the bureaucrats who develop the agencies to hire more bureaucrats who develop more agencies which will require the taxpayers to pay more taxes in order to hire more bureaucrats to develop the increasing number of agencies that will hire more bureaucrats. It is a simple process, and it has been happening to the taxpayers for many years.

of a think tank. While some bureaucrats are known for their marginal thoughts, others are known for effectively tanking up for the think tank. Others can't even swim! In any event, if one is disturbed by a bureaucrat lost in deep thought, one can ask him to turn on his other side.

The Bureaucratic Zoo is the home of many marginal thinkers and many prodigious ponderers. Featherheads can be found in aviaries and program offices while knuckleheads are usually found in reptile buildings and bosses' offices. Birdbrains are more domesticated than featherheads and are rarely seen in aviaries. They make excellent administrators . . . particularly in academic bureaucracies. Pinheads are often housed with loquacious loons, and though they are not mammals, they tend to be preoccupied with mammarial profiles. When permitted to run loose, pinheads often run for public office.

The many species of creatures to be found in the Bureaucratic Zoo have a common fear of being forced into small dark enclosures, and they tremble at the thought of being forced to think. As we wander along the trail of the zoo seeking to find paralogistic wisdom and senilified tranquility, let us avoid posing embarrassing questions that require either facts or decisions. As a distinguished apprentice genius, Vago de los Ríos, once riddled, "Mental tranquility produces celibate concepts nurture political parties dazzle the people give up."

When in trouble, delegate.

Most bureaucrats are open-minded.

Bureaucratic education has nothing to do with the
acquisition of knowledge; it is learning how to appear
to be wise while safeguarding the inner spirit of
mental vacuity.

*Thoughts in a bureaucracy may be either ineffable
or marginal — but never original.*

The wise old men of bureaucracy are those who know where the right memos are buried.

The measurement of the gestation period of an
original thought in a bureaucracy is still pending.

Bureaucratic titillation is more physical than mental . . .
but, of course, it is a subject that needs more study.

Beware of happy bureaucrats. They may know something you don't.

Rumperatory *is a bureaucratic term that applies to the laggistic element of either physical structures or logical abstractions. Rumperatory statements, for example, often reflect the rumbleseat or afterthought of bureaucratic wisdom. Rumperatory abandon may describe how many men think and a few women walk.*

institutional factors

In a bureaucracy it is the *urgency* of a matter, not the *importance,* that determines its priority. Bureaucracy thrives on crisis, and bureaucrats love the thrill of the frenzied flow of paper and the excitement of buzzing conferences. With each crisis come new programs, new agencies, and new taxes.

Let us hypothesize !?!

When bureaucrats discovered that great public concern was developing about the world's environment, their fiscal antennae picked up signals that legislative bodies would make money available to help "meet the crisis." Small meetings began buzzing in governmental agencies at many levels in many governments. "There will be a lot of 'environment' money this year, and we must have program proposals in order to get our piece of the action." This sentiment was echoed in small meetings that grew into bureau-wide meetings that grew into agency task forces.

As governmental bureaucrats drafted their proposals, a similar series of meetings were taking place in many corporate board rooms. The corporate fund-raisers developed proposals for various programs, and all proposals included extra returns in the provisions for overhead costs. The corporate proposals were submitted to government agencies for funding.

Agencies of government and industrial combines worked together to meet "the environment crisis." Small agency offices grew to become bureaus and each soon had its own program funded and in operation. In-house programs were supplemented or combined with corporate programs funded through agency contracts. But the program thrust was orchestrated by many offices and many bureaus that practiced rhetorical coordination and operational isolation.

Subsequent legislative action combined all the environmental activities into a single agency, but all the old agencies continued to maintain liaison offices to work with the new agency.

The energy crisis, the population explosion, and even the crisis of the increasing burden of bureaucratic paperwork have been among the many concerns of an aroused public that have stimulated the growth of offices, commissions and agencies. And they grew . . . and they grow.

Crisis, therefore, is the culture in which bureaucracy grows, and crises shall be with us as long as we have the beat of a single bureaucratic heart.

Let us listen to a few of the throbbing hearts of the Bureaucratic Zoo. If we are nice little visitors, perhaps we may even have a glimpse of one or two organizational charts. At least, if we listen carefully, we may hear a few inspiring mumbles.

While taxpayers sleep bureaucracies grow.

Staff meeting: The pause that depresses.

Some bureaucrats linger at their nests as they seek to hatch fertile ideas and develop promotion-oriented new programs. Many ideas, however, prove to be half-fertile at conception and half-baked at hatching.

I never met a computer that I liked.

*Preliminary research indicates that the cause
of organizational illness can often be traced
to olives and tiny bits of twisted lemon.*

dynamic inaction

Bureaucratic artisans through the ages have known of the beauty that is to be found in dynamic inaction and assured purposelessness. By applying the principles of dynamic inaction and by using decision postponement patterns, the bureaucrats of the world have been able to keep things from happening and thereby have prevented mistakes from being made.

By projecting the image of aggressive leadership while mentally searching for the easiest path to take, bureaucrats have bubbled with cesspoolian movement to the top levels of organizations. By appearing to take bold positions on issues while frantically seeking a safe place to land, bureaucrats have established themselves as outstanding authorities in many fields. By seeming to move steadfastly toward desirable objectives while opening many doors for forward retreat, the practitioners of the bureaucratic art mush through life with haughty confidence in their disdainful ignorance.

The beauty of dynamic inaction has been expressed in the paintings of men and women who have captured the inner spirit of bureaucratic life. The devoted use of bureaucracy's official colors, gray on gray, reflects keen insights into the neutral nature of goal-oriented purposelessness.

Composers have captured the spirit of dynamic inaction in the joyous dirges to which all bureaucrats must march, and poets have grasped the range of bureaucratic values in their single-minded sonnets. The orbital dialogues that are used to fuzzify issues, the steadfast yesbuttisms that weave the acceptable patterns of decision postponement, and the pulsating vitality of nondirective logic have characterized the life style of successful bureaucrats.

These artistic expressions are appropriately harmonized with the resonance of philosophical murmurings. The earliest murmurings about dynamic inaction can be traced to the *Tao Teh King* in which Lao-Tse, the great philosopher of the sixth century B.C., wrote inspiring words-to-mumble. Lao-Tse wrote:

A state may be ruled by measures of correction;
weapons of war may be used with crafty dexterity;
but the kingdom is made one's own only by freedom
from action and purpose.

Freedom from action and freedom from purpose constitute the philosophical bases of creative bureaucracy.

In the new bureaucratic institutions or in old institutions that have new leadership, there may be temporary periods of activity. Occasionally a new bureaucrat may have the ridiculous idea that he is supposed to do something merely because he is in charge[1]. Or, an old-timer may get excited and forget that action of any type may disturb the tranquility of the ship of state. These lapses, however, are infrequent and usually result in little more than supportive editorials in the media and knowing acknowledgment from taxpayers.

---

1. The masculine pronoun is used not necessarily to reflect chauvinistic tendencies, but because the author believes that women make poor bureaucrats. Women have not learned to play the bureaucratic game; they tend to insist on answers to questions and to move diligently toward the resolution, not the study, of problems.

If you want to stop something or be told why you can't do something you don't want to do, ask General Counsel for an opinion. Their wisdom is exceeded only by their speed.

When in charge, ponder.

Nothing is impossible until it is sent to a committee.

Most bureaucrats serve other bureaucrats.

Upon receiving the Ph.D. degree, many academic bureaucrats wrap their brains in cobwebs and settle down to mental retirement. Some start earlier and become administrators.

When you see two bureaucrats engaged in quiet conversation, do not disturb them. They may be knitting their wits.

*Beginning bureaucrats who are frustrated by
procedural abstractions and elusive logic are often
roaring wall-climbers. The passage of time and the
accumulation of scars, however, usually convert
wall-climbers into hibernating salary collectors.*

In a bureaucracy, sitting is safer than running and sleeping is safer than doing.

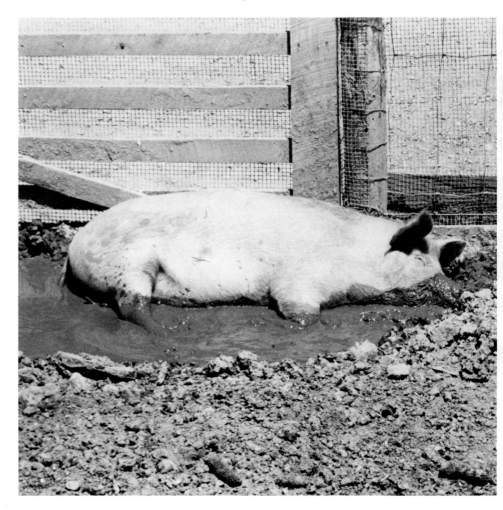

Bureaucratic consistency does not refer to consistency of policy but to viscosity of substance. And regardless of viscosity, most bureaucrats are excellent swimmers and waders.

In bureaucracies there is to be found no such thing as a virginal bureaucrat. Bureaucratic virgins there may be, but virginal bureaucrats there will never be, because the very nature of the give-and-take relationship between bureaucrats and taxpayers make it an impossibility.

Bureaucratic virgins may retain their status for extended periods of time because of personal values, but *personal* values have very little influence on *institutional* values and practices. These institutional values and practices are important in the growth and development of bureaucrats. Life in a bureaucracy, of course, ultimately makes clearance procedures and feasibility studies vital elements in the bureaucrats' approach to everything; clearances and studies are the principal tools that enable bureaucrats to postpone decisions and to control the birth of ideas. The celibate concepts and the indecision to be found in the Bureaucratic Zoo are protective shields that enable all bureaucratic species to survive.[1]

---

1. Bureaucrats are pleased at the rapid growth of the bureaucratic movement, but they recognize two problems related to taxpayer support and the population explosion.

As more and more bureaucrats join the bureaucracy there are fewer taxpayers to support them. The International Association of Professional Bureaucrats has urged a world-wide tax reform program that would give tax incentives to the decreasing number of taxpayers to encourage them to work harder to support the increasing number of those who do not work.

Bureaucrats are concerned about the rapid growth of the world's population, but, of course, do not want to be forced to make decisions that may have moral implications. The world's population explosion can be solved while avoiding the moral issue of abortion by applying an orchestration of personal and institutional celibacy known as the Boren Formula for Population Control (BoFoFoPopCon). Under BoFoFoPopCon a massive
(Continued)

In-house relationships between bureaucrats in the executive branch rarely have sexual overtones; their relationships are more commonly those of buddies . . . or, perhaps, acupuncturing buddibirds. In-house relationships between political or legislative bureaucrats, on the other hand, may have apartmental influences which can cause buddibirds to be replaced by nocturnal nightygales or moulting bed-thrashers. The relative size of the legislative or political bureaucracies as compared with the size of executive or administrative bureaucracies, however, makes the behavioral patterns around legislative halls somewhat minimal in their influence.

Institutionally, it may be said that the relationship between the world's second oldest profession, bureaucracy, and the world's oldest profession is rather marginal. Personal marketing is more commonly practiced than institutional marketing, and in-house commerce is rarely physcal. *Bureaucrats rarely have sex with one another. What they do, they do to the public.* The process is rather simple, straightforward, and has no pornographic implications.

Pornography to a bureaucrat is a blank sheet of paper. Whereas some people make occasional or regular visits to

1. (Continued)
research program would be launched to find a way to double the human gestation period from nine to eighteen months. To be successful, it would be merely necessary to teach Mother Nature what is known about governmental programming techniques, clearance procedures, and study committee operations. With Mother Nature using established bureaucratic practices, the human gestation period would be doubled and perhaps tripled. The implications of BoFoFoPopCon are being studied by a standing committee of the International Association of Professional Bureaucrats (INATAPROBU) and the Department of Chauvinist Studies, Washington Faculty, Peter University.

book stores that have painted or curtained windows, professional bureaucrats prefer to browse in office supply stores, print shops, and other places that produce or display the working tools and playthings of happy bureaucrats. The happy bureaucrat knows how to hook, and the sensuous bureaucrat knows how to sow. For it is the hooking of taxpayers and the sowing of sheets of paper, six-part forms, and copies of new regulations that give the greatest joy to happy and sensuous bureaucrats.

The sounds of the Bureaucratic Zoo, therefore, are more paperistic than cooistic; the dances are more shufflistic than matistic; the colors are more perceived than real; and the sex is more conversational than functional. Neutrality of color, neutrality of sound, and neutrality of dynamism enable the creatures of the Bureaucratic Zoo to keep a low profile and quietly survive.

To truly understand the sex habits of bureaucrats, of course, it is best to observe them at work and play. For some it is an obligation to help preserve the species, but for others it is merely the joy of giving.

Never now.

Bureaucrats rarely have sex with one another.
What they do, they do to the public.

Sunrise is a beautiful time of day . . .
unless you're just arriving home.

If one wishes to have fun and also practice natural birth control, one should have a bureaucrat as a partner. Bureaucrats are great on procedures and low on production.

Bureaucrats make poor lovers because they insist on making feasibility studies at every step of the way.

Male chauvinist bureaucrats are usually broadminded—
when they are not having to think of other things.

philosophical mumblings

The pursuit of wisdom is rarely found in bureaucracies, because bureaucrats are too busy developing the image of being wise to give time to the pursuit of wisdom itself. Professional bureaucrats know that people can perceive an image easier than they can perceive reality, and people will accept the minimessages of press releases more quickly than substantive and thought-provoking messages.

People do not like to be thought-provoked, and bureaucrats are happy to accommodate them. It is easier; it is safer; and, sometimes the bureaucrats can't do anything else anyway.

The progress of individual bureaucrats, however, is rarely related to the progress of the bureaucracies in which they work. Institutions do not exist for the purpose of doing anything other than the nurturing of bureaucrats. They are the nesting areas about which all bureaucrats may grumble but for which all bureaucrats will fight if endangered by some outside force. By providing the proper care and feeding of bureaucrats, the bureaucracies grow and grow.

The growth and progress of bureaucracies are puffistically flaqued by public affairs officers and advertising agencies. Their reports are usually issued immediately prior to corporate board meetings, legislative investigations, or alumni fund-raising drives. An implemented banality is often the basis of a bureaucracy's progress report.

All bureaucrats seek to move up the career ladder. The motivation may be more money; it may be more power; or, it may be for purposes of status. It is rarely, however, motivated by a desire for additional responsibility. Some bureaucrats get ahead by plodding, others by plotting. The plod-plot axis is usually tilted in favor of the plotters, and the plodders get the short end of the stick. This is known as the bureaucratic shaft.

Politicians always express concern about the way their constituents are treated by the bureaucracies over which they have legislative or executive jurisdiction but with which they have reached a comfortable accommodation. Bureaucrats understand the game, and as election-year oratory places bureaucracy in the bull's-eye of its cyclical target, knowledgeable bureaucrats merely residuate both for visual and auditory low profiles. Reorganization of bureaucracy has been a rhetorical concern of vote-seeking politicians since the first hand was raised in an oratorical stance.

Bureaucrats are never afraid of reorganization. They know that a time of reorganization is a time to quietly sit, prodigiously ponder, and patiently pulsate. Historical mumblings have indicated that bureaucratic expansion always follows reorganizational initiatives. For example, the Boren Plan for reorganizing the national units of government call for a beginning at the grass-roots level. The Boren Plan would consolidate while appearing to decentralize. It's nothing new; it has been done many times.

First, more authority would appear to be delegated to the states or provinces. Second, all states and provinces would be consolidated into two states. The old units, of course, continue to exist for patronage and office-holding purposes, but the two new structures would layerize an additional level that would provide the basis for even more jobs and more taxes. The crisis of bureaucratic growth would thus be solved by bureaucratic growth.

Presidents, prime ministers, governors, mayors and legislative bodies always attack the problem of bureaucracy by setting up study commissions. The study commissions study previous studies, review reviews of previous studies, and review the reviews of previous reviews. If time permits before the next election is held, surveys of reviews of reviews of previous reviews can be initiated. Study commissions are established to postpone decisions, minimize actions, and preserve the *status quo*. Bureaucrats, therefore, are never worried about demands for bureaucratic reorganization. They know it is the election cycle, and they look forward to new opportunities for institutional proliferation.

Historically, the wisdom of the ages has been sanitized by the transmitters of the wisdom. The bureaucrats are the record keepers, the chroniclers of history. Just as the Incas had their keepers of the quipu to record their inventories, and just as the Incas had their "rememberers" to remember what they wanted remembered, senior level bureaucrats have their "keepers of the memos." They can extract those memos that reflect the wisdom of their actions and shred those that may reflect minimal brilliance.

The pursuit of wisdom in a bureaucracy, therefore, is not a philosophical matter. It is an adjustivity of wisdom that will enhance the public image of bureaucrats and their institutions. In a bureaucracy, goals are to be stated, not sought; actions are to be studied, not taken; and, knowledge is to be synthesized, not used.

The lion, the King of Beasts, shall reign in the Bureaucratic Zoo with loud and majestic pronouncements of reorganizing the kingdom. His reign shall be supreme . . . until the winds of change announce the arrival of the skunk.[1]

---

1. Insightfully Hammarskjoldian.

The corporate canatopsis

So work that when thy summons comes to face
Thy corporate board of directors that moves
In that mysterious realm, where each must take
His chances on survival's firing line,
Thou go not, like a bureaucrat in fear,
Bound in his red tape, but, sustained and soothed
By a semantical trust, approach thy board
Like one who wraps the fuzziness of his words
About him, and preserves the status quo.

An effective way to deflate a pompous bureaucrat is through the use of a rectal thermometer. Of course, it may be necessary to tell the bureaucrat how to use it.

The Boren Dictum: *If you're going to be a phoney,*
be sincere about it.

*The safest time for a beginner in a game of chess
or in a bureaucracy is when the beginner is waiting
for the opponent's first move.*

There once was a time when government waste referred to money.

*No greater fear hath a bureaucrat than the fear
of being discovered or of losing a parking place.*

*Recognition of one's own ignorance immediately
disqualifies one from becoming a congressman,
a college dean, or a bureaucrat.*

Truth to the bureaucrat is the latest regulation.

The bureaucrat who tries to get credit for everything eventually will.

You can always tell the difference between a professional bureaucrat and a beginning bureaucrat.
The professional never snores.

Taxes are for poor people.

the forward look

History
is the
forward look
of contemporary
bureaucrats.

ThE SEARCh FOR
ThE ULTiMATE MUMBLE

A Look to the Future

With pad and pencil in hand, with tape recorder hanging from my belt, and with my research associates struggling to keep pace with my waddlistic pursuits, I have traveled the trails of the world's bureaucratic jungles, and have studied the behavior of the creatures of the bureaucratic zoo. I pondered the principles of dynamic inaction, the marginality of thought processes, the nondirectiveness of orbital dialogues, the fuzzification of viable options, and the profundification of simple concepts. I sought to gain all the knowledge and master all the skills that related directly and indirectly to bureaucracy.

As I moved around the world in quest of that knowledge, however, the nature of the search gradually changed into pursuit of a single unmatched expression of the bureaucratic way of life. As Diogenes carried his lantern as he searched for an honest man, so did I carry my bureaucratic tools to record The Ultimate Mumble.

In Washington I moved quietly down the halls of the State Department Building in search of the mumble to end all mumbles. Though known as the campus of the Graduate School of the Mumbling Arts, the quiet halls and somniferous conference rooms of the State Department did not reveal The Ultimate Mumble. I found only the multiple echoes of single syllable thoughts. In the Pentagon, I found five-sided mumbles to support training programs that statistically had almost two instructors for every trainee, and whose educational technology had been crystallized shortly after World War II. The fresh mumbles found in the Environmental Protection Agency dealt with guidelines on the use of cancer-causing chemicals, but the mumbles were muffled in EPA's television studio whose ceiling was soundproofed by two inches of cancer-causing asbestos. In the Fertile Valley of the Potomac, I found a great multiphonic marshalling of tones that were mumbled to the accompaniment of political woodwinds, bureaucratic drummers, lobbying brass, and White House strings.

I sought to find the supernal mumble in Ottawa where I crawled beneath the angular and tubular sculptures that stand as centurions before the magnificent Buildings of State. But I found only an admixture of bilingual tonalities that, as inspiring as they were, did not configurate with Gestaltic finality the beauty of a major mumble. From Ottawa I shuffled to St. John's and Halifax . . . thence to Toronto, Winnipeg, and Victoria, but I found that, contrary to popular conception, the mumbling was more newfified in Toronto than in other zoos of Canada . . . including St. John's. Even the best bilingual newfifications, however, did not meet the test for the great mumble.

The long shadows of the Tower of London, the soapboxed corners of Hyde Park, the resonating chamber of The Albert Hall, and the magnificent Halls of Parliament were the nesting places of great mumblers, but the mumbling did not meet the test of the big one. How disappointing it was to waddle along the trails where the great English wafflers waffled only to find that in the home of my mother tongue the mumbling, though delightfully accented, was primarily loopily loud, dolefully dull, and staidly sterile!

In Brasilia I crawled under the closed dome of the Senate, and I waded through the open bowl of the House. I learned that the happy mumbling was to be found when the nocturnal zoo was punctuated by the quiet dialogues of boa boas and irreversible jaetos. The singing mumbles of the great Brazilian zoo were rhythmic in joyous sounds, but they failed to produce the euphonious tones of The Ultimate Mumble.

The shrill sounds of Cairo; the resinous tincturizations of Athens; the umpahs of Bonn; the ramblisms of Rome; the third language of Kingston; the embromazations of Lima, La Paz, and Caracas; the lilting tones of Santiago and Tegucigalpa; the mariachification of Mexico City; the marathon sounds of Tokyo, Hong Kong, and Bangkok; the twangistic patterns of Austin and Oklahoma City; the feathery tones of Atlanta, Jackson, and Columbia; the crispy clip of Augusta and Boston; the verbal foggifications of Olympia and Sacramento . . . These and the characteristics of other beautiful zoos throughout the world were among those studied as I searched for the big mumble of mumbles.

But, alas! The search was not fulfilled.

Having failed to find The Ultimate Mumble in world-wide travels to the great Bureaucratic Zoos, and having unsuccessfully carried the search through all levels of governmental, corporate and academic bureaucracies, I began to turn the search to the biggest of the big pictures. Perhaps it's not merely a world-wide zoo . . . perhaps it's a zoo of the universe . . . Just maybe . . .

"Eureka," I shouted to the trees of my beloved mountain, "I may have it! Yes, I may have discovered The Ultimate Mumble . . . the mumble to end all mumbles . . . the last of the red hot mumbles!"

Suddenly I was overcome with a strange sensation that seemed to blend the joy of discovery with the sadness of what the discovery could really mean. The sadness soon ruled over the last twinge of joy, and through tearful eyes and ringing ears, I saw the vision and heard the sound of what I thought was The Ultimate Mumble.

It was the earth that I viewed through a tearful haze as I

mentally floated on an ethereal speck of spatial dust. In the vision I saw the earth as a great mass of pulsating and writhing red tape—red tape that covered the globe in loose but tenacious entanglement. As I gazed unbelievingly upon the strange scene, I saw one human hand as it tremblingly reached outward through the maze of ribbons as if making a last feeble grasp for reality.

I saw the earth as it shuddered in its orbit, and I heard the eerie and loudly creaking sound as it began to cease to rotate on its axis. Suddenly there came a thunderously shattering sound . . . one that would crash through the sound barriers of all eternity. It was the last rasping, grating creak as the world, like all its bureaucratic institutions through the ages, ground to a halt.

Stunned by the vision of what I had witnessed and the sound of what I had heard, I watched as the earth, in its ribbons of red, began to slowly and silently drift away. Could the final creaking sound of the earth with its burden of red tape be The Ultimate Mumble?

"No! " I shouted as I shook my head to free it from the mental cobwebs of the vision. "No, The Ultimate Mumble is not a sound of sadness. It must be a sound of happiness!"

What, then, is the mumbling sound for which I have searched around the world? Or, is it a sound itself? Could it be the mere *echo* of an original sound? Yes, perhaps, but . . .

Never in history has a bureaucrat been known to have second thoughts about anything. By definition it is an impossibility. Since no originalities have been found in the hystorical study of bureaucracy, must all echoes be the echoes of third-generation mumbles? My mind was spinning in spiraling confusion!

Of course, it is possible to have original *sounds* without original *thoughts*. But original sounds are mushified in their tonalities, fuzzified in their definitions, and profundified in their ineffable notes.

Can the echo of a sound be louder and more profound than an original sound? In the unreal world in which people live, no; but in the real world of bureaucracy, perhaps yes! Ah, but an echo would not have the full majesty and authoritative resonance of The Ultimate Mumble.

With such marginal thoughts moving with dizzying speed through my mind, I strolled to the original path that I had taken as I launched my search for The Ultimate Mumble. The sounds of the Bureaucratic Zoo were everywhere as I paused in my stroll to sit on a curb with elbows on my knees and head in my hands. My ears and mind then began to function in harmony as I heard a strange new brand of sounds. Words? Phrases? Some new species with a new system of communicating?

I tried to filter out all other sounds and thoughts to concentrate on the cracklings and sputterings that I heard coming from a government vehicle stopped at a nearby traffic signal.

"Hello, ole buddy, this is Budget Breaker here, alookin' over your left shoulder where I gotcha on a big nine. That's a negatory on the cotton pickin' tax cut, ole buddy, that's a negatory. We gotta eighteen wheeler on the committee and a classified wrapper on the spendin' level, so bear down, ole buddy, bear down. We got a clear on the spendin' and we're gonna find that big ole rockin' chair we been alookin' for. And that's a ten-four for shore, ole buddy, that's a ten-four for shore."

Can this be it? Is this The Ultimate Mumble that has evolved from the philosophy of Socrates, Plato, and Aristotle? Is this the final influence of Shakespeare, Browning, and Dickinson? Can I visualize a proud smile on the face of a Winston Churchill as he ringingly proclaims, "Ten-four, ole buddy, ten-four!"?

Mmmmmmmm. Maybe I'll try again tomorrow........